ROMANTIC SCOTLAND

ROMANTIC SCOTLAND

Charles Maclean

Photographs by
Fritz von der Schulenburg

Weidenfeld and Nicolson
London

Text © Charles Maclean 1994
Photographs © Fritz von der Schulenburg 1994
Photograph on page 57 courtesy of Abercrombie & Kent Ltd

First published in Great Britain in 1994
by George Weidenfeld & Nicolson Limited,
Orion House, 5, Upper St. Martin's Lane,
London WC2H 9EA

This edition first published in 1996

British Library Cataloguing in Publication Data
A catalogue for this book is available from the British Library

Designed by Ronald Clark
Map by M L Design
Printed and bound in Italy

Half-title page::
Powder horn, framed print and sword at Strachur House

Frontispiece:
Creag Meagaidh

For Rosie and Shimi, Charlotte and Rhoda

Acknowledgements
The authors would like to thank all the owners of the houses and gardens
that appear in this book for allowing them to be photographed. We are
particularly grateful to Mrs Patricia and Jean Maxwell Scott, Sir Donald
Cameron of Lochiel, Sir Fitzroy Maclean of Dunconnel and Mrs R. Ward
for their help and hospitality. We are also greatly indebted to the organizing
skills of Karen Howes, who assisted Fritz von der Schulenburg on his
travels throughout the length and breadth of Scotland, collated the
photographic materail and generally created order and light where
creative chaos tended to reign.

CONTENTS

Shetlands

Fetlar

LERWICK ●

0 10 20 30 40 miles

0 10 20 30 40 50 60 km

Orkneys

Earl's Palace ■

Mainland

Stenness ●

Old Man of Hoy ●

Hoy

Scapa Flow

Churchill Barrier ●

Lewis

Cranstackie (2630 ft) △

Loch Eriboll

● Tongue

THURSO ●

WICK ●

Loch Glencoul

Strath of Kildonan

River Helmsdale

Kildonan ●

Berriedale ●

Helmsdale ●

Dunrobin Castle ■

Little Loch Broom

Loch Broom

ULLAPOOL ●

Dornoch Firth

Tarbat Ness

Harris

Dundonnell House ●

Corrieshalloch Gorge

Moray Firth

Ben Wyvis (3433 ft) △

North Uist

W E S T E R   R O S S

Cromarty ●

The Falls of Rogie ●

Strathpeffer ●

Black Isle

Castle Stuart ■

Culloden ✕

Cawdor Castle ■

River Beauly

INVERNESS ●

Skye

Loch Carron

Plockton ●

Glen Urquhart

River Spey

Dufftown ●

Glenlivet

Loanhead Stone Circle ■

South Uist

CUILLIN HILLS

Boat of Garten ●

Corgarff Castle ■

Craigievar Castle ■

Loch Ness

Aviemore ●

ABERDEEN ●

Barra

INTRODUCTION

Glencoe

Celebrated for its magnificent, even awesome scenery and its rich historical associations, Glencoe ('Glen of Weeping') leads from Rannoch Moor in Argyll to Loch Leven on the west coast of Inverness-shire. High among the Three Sisters of Glencoe (*left*), lies Ossian's Cave, the legendary birthplace of the third-century Gaelic bard. Another more genuine landmark is the Signal Rock, near Clachaig Inn, allegedly from where the signal to begin the infamous massacre of the MacDonalds of Glencoe was given on the night of 13 February 1692. On the orders of William III and the Master of Stair, who wanted to make an example of a Jacobite clan in their drive to control the Highlands, the massacre was carried out by Campbell of Glenlyon and 128 soldiers, who had been living for several days on friendly terms with the MacDonalds. They killed forty of their hosts, men, women and children, and drove others off into the snow to die of exposure and want. The cruelty of the deed resonates to this day in Scotland.

O Caledonia! stern and wild,
Meet nurse for a poetic child!
Land of brown heath and shaggy wood,
Land of the mountain and the flood,
Land of my sires! what mortal hand
Can e'er untie the filial band,
That knits me to thy rugged strand!

SIR WALTER SCOTT
The Lay of the Last Minstrel

'On returning to Abbotsford,' Walter Scott's son-in-law and biographer, John Lockhart, wrote in 1818, '[we] found Mrs Scott and her daughters doing penance under the merciless curiosity of a couple of tourists . . . they were rich specimens, tall lanky young men both of them rigged out in new jackets and trowsers of the Macgregor tartan'. The visitors, a lawyer and a unitarian preacher from New England, were hoping to catch a glimpse of the world-famous author of *Rob Roy* scribbling away at his desk. Their intrusion was rewarded if not welcomed by Scott, who, cheerfully paying the price of his celebrity, lavished hospitality on all who beat a path to Abbotsford's portcullised gates. His extraordinary popular success as a poet and historical novelist had by then made him a national institution and Abbotsford, his beloved country estate by the banks of the Tweed, an essential place of pilgrimage on the road to the Highlands. For it was here in his book-lined study that the Wizard of the North conjured up the stirring images of Scotland which brought the first droves of tourists north of the border. They came in their thousands eager to see for themselves the dramatic settings of *Waverley* and *Redgauntlet*, ready to be moved to tears by the sublime scenery described in *The Lady of the Lake*, and hoping to be beguiled by the mists of romance that swirled, and swirl still, about Caledonia's 'rugged strand' – and grateful exchequer.

One can picture those early American 'Macgregors', little different from their modern counterparts slung about with Nikons, traipsing through the great baronial pile Scott literally dreamed into existence on the proceeds of his writing. They must have stood, as one stands now, in Abbotsford's 'mediaeval' entrance hall, gazing up at the gleaming array of heroic relics, suits of armour, heraldic shields and grim battlefield trove that Scott collected and which represents, identifiably, the raw material of his fiction. Here hangs Rob Roy's dirk, there the keys with which Mary Queen of Scots' lover helped her escape from Loch Leven Castle; a glass case in the library shows Flora Macdonald's embroidered pocket book lying next to a desiccated morsel of oatcake found in the sporran of a Highlander fallen at Culloden. The cumulative effect of so many romantic curios seems as artificial as the stage set for a Donizetti opera, but Scott's passionate historicism was not so much a quest for authenticity as for inspiration. Although his novels have long since fallen from fashion, their idealized portrayal of Scotland's dramatic landscapes and violent history – the elemental threat of the wilderness sublimated, the blood-stained centuries safely enshrined in legend – gave his country an emotional glamour it has never lost.

When we think of Scotland today, what first comes to mind (thanks largely to Sir Walter Scott, 1771–1832) is a picture of the Highlands. Never mind that the Lowlands – only marginally less high than the Highlands – cover half the country and contain nine-tenths of its population. The imagination flies to the wilder, nobler prospect of Highland hills, where the air is keen and clear, the waters of rushing burn or mountain loch pure enough to bottle and the only sign of human habitation a ruined keep or lone croft (impeccably whitewashed and slate-roofed) standing at the head of a fairy-green glen. Onto this magnificent backcloth project a stag or two browsing the purple heather, fade in the mewing of a golden eagle or the distant skirl of bagpipes, and supply for the foreground, spread on a tartan rug, a picnic of cold salmon, grouse, oatcakes smothered with crowdie, shortbread and the indispensable flask of whisky – and you have every visitor, exile and many a native's dream of Bonnie Scotland.

Abbotsford

Sir Walter Scott built Abbotsford between 1818 and 1824 on the proceeds of his writing, composing the mock gothic, many-turreted mansion by instalments – a wing or floor for each best-selling novel. A highly eccentric building, reflecting Scott's complex personality and eclectic taste, mixing domestic comfort with a one-man revival of the ancient Scottish baronial style, it had an influence on the development of Victorian taste that like the fashion for Scott's novels was international. The entrance hall at Abbotsford reveals the delight Scott took in surrounding himself with Scottish relics. The skull on the mantelpiece is a model of Robert the Bruce's; the basket grate belonged to Archbishop Sharp, murdered on Magus Muir in 1679; the cannonballs are said to have been used at the 1460 siege of Roxburgh Castle – all displayed exactly as he left them in this shrine to Scotland's romantic but violent past.

Abbotsford

The plain, booklined study, with its gallery and hidden staircase leading to his bedroom, allowed Scott to retire into the world of his imagination. More than any room at Abbotsford, it evokes the novelist's presence and bears witness to the monastic demands of his profession. Yet, engagingly, Scott had a very modest opinion of his literary powers. A sociable, family-minded man, he considered writing a means rather than an end and was never happier than when playing the role of Border Laird, wandering about his estate with a permanent entourage of friends, dependents and devoted dogs. Faced with sudden and complete financial ruin at the age of fifty-five, Scott implemented the heroic decision to write his way out of debt. In six years he earned £80,000 with his pen and, though the effort killed him, he managed to save his beloved Abbotsford for his children.

What is revealing about this technicoloured view of the Highlands is not so much that it's inaccurate or sentimental – even the most extravagant description cannot outrival the scenery – or that it ignores the hardship and misery that throughout history has too often been the Highlander's lot, but that it reflects the modern tendency to equate the whole of Scotland with its poorest, emptiest region. Ironically, 250 years ago the exact reverse was the case: Scotland then meant only the Lowlands. The mountainous waste that lay to the north and west was regarded as a separate country, where any traveller (even, or particularly, if a Lowland Scot) was advised to take the precaution of making his will before venturing. As late as 1773, when Boswell escorted Dr Johnson on their famous tour, the greater part of the Highlands remained an unknown wilderness. The view from London and Edinburgh alike was of an alien territory no less remote than the wilds of Afghanistan and in-fested with savage tribes that had only recently been subdued. Thirty years after the defeat of Bonnie Prince Charlie at Culloden, the kilt was still proscribed in Scotland as 'the garb of sedition'. Yet by the end of the eighteenth century the dangers had been forgotten, the power of the clans smashed with the consequent grudging merger of Highlands and Lowlands, and tartan (as worn by once proud warlike chiefs) become all the rage in London, Paris, even New York: the fashion for the Highlands that would reach its climax in the reign of Queen Victoria had caught on.

If a single event can be said to have inspired the idea of romantic Scotland, even before Robert Burns complained that his heart was in the Highlands, and not here, the distinction must go to the publication in 1760 of the *Poems of Ossian*. Presented as the lost effusions of an archaic west coast bard, discovered and translated from the Gaelic by James Macpherson (1736–96), an unknown Inverness schoolteacher with a literary bent, the Ossianic sagas retold the misty legends and folk tales of the Highlands and Islands in high-flown language that skilfully evoked the elemental grandeur of their storm-lashed locales. The authenticity of the poems was immediately questioned by, among others, Dr Johnson, who demonstrated that although loosely based on fragments of Celtic myth and legendry, the verses of Ossian were Macpherson's own composition. Doubts over provenance notwithstanding – Macpherson was never able to produce an original manuscript to back his claim – the impact of Ossian's primitive and sentimental poetry on Europe and its fledgling Romantic movement was extraordinary. The epic of *Fingal*, one of the most widely admired and imitated works in the history of literature, captured the imaginations of Goethe, Herder and later Felix Mendelssohn, who visited Fingal's Cave on Staffa to find inspiration for his haunting 'Hebrides' overture. Ossian's enthusiastic reception by the major poets, writers and composers of the age, including Schiller, Blake, Diderot, Scott, Byron, Massenet and most of the nineteenth-century French Romantics, raised Macpherson from obscurity to being for half a century the most influential poet in Europe. His rhapsodic celebration of the Highland scene had likewise put Scotland on the map, not only creating the idea of Gaeldom as a place of infinite romance, but making it the spiritual theme park of the Romantic movement itself.

The Ossianic fever that gripped Europe even awakened the interest of the English in their long-feared and despised northern neighbour. Among the first visitors to Scotland after the claymores of the '45 Rebellion had been safely sheathed was Dr Johnson, who, in his *Journey to the Western Islands of Scotland*, declared himself no more taken by the bleak and barren country he travelled through than by its barbarous inhabitants. 'The finest prospect a Scotsman will ever behold', he pronounced, 'is the highroad that leads to England.' An earlier traveller, John English, had been even less complimentary, but the rapturous accounts of dramatic scenery and hospitable natives by Thomas Pennant and other eighteenth-century travel writers were more persuasive. In an age that extolled the virtues of the Noble Savage, the idea of simple, warm-hearted folk eking out poor but honest lives dignified by the natural majesty of their surroundings outweighed the discomforts of the voyage and made the Highlands an irresistibly exotic destination.

Travel in the North may have lost its outlandish allure, but the modern visitor's expectations of Scotland have hardly changed. The promise of unspoilt countryside and unspoilt people, cast in the nostalgic glow of *Brigadoon*, *Whisky Galore* or *Dr Findlay's Casebook*, continues to draw Southrons to isolated villages and misty islands. If there's a risk of finding the locals outnumbered by 'white settlers' – the Isle of Mull, for instance, has become as overgrown with retired colonels and bank managers as Tunbridge Wells – one can still be reasonably sure of experiencing aspects of traditional Highland life that do not do violence to cherished stereotypes. The hospitality for which the Highlands have long been famous may be a legacy of clannish pride and sanguinary codes of honour, but the bonds of kinship that formed the bedrock of Celtic society have proved no less durable than the Anglo-Saxon preoccupation with class. The natives remain proud but friendly; the welcoming conviviality of Highlanders, their unstrained warmth, the luxury they enjoy of being at ease in their own skins afforded by knowing who they are, lending sustenance and substance to the romantic myth.

In the heyday of the clans, the Highlands rivalled the Balkans as a place of simmering conflicts and shifting alliances where treachery and danger were ever present. The clan chiefs were little different than Chetnik warlords, as contemptuous of government as they were bloodily reliant on the economics of plunder, yet we prefer to see them now as heroic, the splendid defenders of a fierce but doomed independence. Who but a Highland chief would have had his steward proclaim from the battlements of Kisimul Castle, with only the seals and seagulls for an audience: 'Hear ye people, and listen ye nations. The great Macneil of Barra having finished his meal, the princes of the earth may now dine'? If such hubristic nonsense can engage our sympathy, it's partly because with hindsight we recognize in Macneil's magnificent challenge (to a world that had never heard of him) the melancholy shadow cast over the history of the clans by the ill-fated Jacobite rebellions. Already an anachronism at the outset of the eighteenth century, the clan system did not survive the debacle suffered by the Stuart army at Culloden in 1746. On that desolate moorland, where the mass graves of individual clans are still marked with rough weather-worn stones, the Highlanders died for their own lost cause, as well as for Prince Charlie's, going down in charge after charge of hopeless gallantry that as no victory could have done set the heather ablaze with legends of glory and pity.

One of the world's great romantic adventures, the '45, or Charlie's Year, as it was known in Scotland, helped form our modern attitude to the Highlands. After Culloden, the brutal Hanoverian efficiency with which the Duke of Cumberland punished the clans loyal to Bonnie Prince Charlie – putting the countryside to 'fire and sword', forfeiting clan lands, stripping the chiefs of their powers and banning them along with their clansmen from wearing tartan or carrying weapons – produced a revulsion of feeling that duly made martyrs of the Highlanders. As a determined effort to eradicate the Highland menace, it succeeded; the spirit of the clans was broken, the old way of life gone forever; but the sense of wrong done to a people lingered on, keeping alive a flame that might otherwise have blown itself out. In the aftermath of the rebellion, the destruction wreaked by Cumberland's troops was compounded by economic hardship and, after a brief period of relative prosperity, a population explosion that led among other drastic solutions (adopted too often by the Highland chiefs themselves) to wholesale evictions and forced emigration. The tragedy of the Clearances, the removal of people to make room for sheep and game, left another deep scar on the Highlands still visible today in far and empty glens where the grass ghosts of cultivation ridges or a few heaps of stone bear poignant witness to an abandoned clachan or settlement. But the wrenching of the Highlander from his ancestral lands also opened up another rich seam of pathos and sentiment and created an audience of exiles abroad with an insatiable appetite for songs, poetry and paintings that gave a nostalgic, often idealized view of home. In the anonymous lament of a nineteenth-century exile to Canada, the voice of the disinherited has retained all of its emotional force:

> From the lone shieling of the misty island
> Mountains divide us, and the waste of seas;
> Yet still the blood is strong, the heart is Highland
> And we in dreams behold the Hebrides.
> When the bold kindred, in the time long-vanish'd,
> Conquer'd the soil and fortified the keep,
> No seer foretold the children would be banish'd,
> That a degenerate lord might boast his sheep.

Isle of Skye

Until the last war almost half the croft houses in the Hebrides were based on the indigenous 'black house' design. Only a few black houses are still inhabited today, and most of these are conversions like the one pictured here. While a certain stigma still attaches to its 'primitiveness', the black house was built to withstand the rigours of the climate. Low to the ground, its streamlined, immensely thick walls were packed with a mixture of peat and gravel for insulation. The rounded thatch roof, held in place by ropes made of twisted heather and stone weights, reached only to the inner wall, leaving no eaves to be caught by the wind. Water drained into the cavity material between the walls, keeping it moist and draught-proof. A small hole in the roof allowed some light to penetrate and smoke to escape from the peat fire kept in day and night on a central hearth; it was from the dark, soot-blackened, smoky interior that the black house took its name.

Glenfinlas Street, Edinburgh

By the mid-eighteenth century, Edinburgh had grown in population, prosperity and reputation to the extent that its more well-to-do citizens living in the overcrowded mediaeval warren of the Old Town felt the need to expand. In 1767 a decision was made to extend the city northwards and a plan to build a New Town across the ravine (then the water-filled Nor' Loch) according to the inspired design of a twenty-three-year-old architect, James Craig, was put into action. The work of expansion was continued well into the nineteenth century by a number of architects, including William Playfair and J.G. Graham; the result, a well laid out grid of wide streets, fine town houses and graceful crescents and squares, has been admired the world over. Glenfinlas Street leads out of the north-west corner of Charlotte Square, which was designed and partly built by Robert Adam and along its north side has few equals anywhere.

Of those who lost everything but stayed behind, some joined the newly formed Highland regiments, others turned to crofting, each in their different ways upholding the fragmented traditions of the Highlands. While many a foreign field resounded to the martial clatter of pipes and drums, crofters at home struggled to wrest a precarious living from marginal land that would have otherwise reverted to wilderness. A self-sufficient way of life, harsh yet rewarding, crofting extended both the viability of remote townships and the survival of the primitive rubble-walled and turf-roofed 'black house', the indigenous form of rural Scottish architecture, which up until 1940 accounted for almost half the dwellings in the Outer Isles. Crofting also helped to preserve (as did the Highland regimental tradition and the churches in Scotland) something of the old independent yet communal character of the Highlands and Islands with its rich heritage of legends, beliefs, historical associations, poetry and music. The devout origins of this sense of community reach back at least to the time of St Columba and the early Christian settlements up and down the west coast, but most importantly on Iona, for a century or more the centre of Christian Europe. Today, if one can escape the crowds of pilgrims and tourists milling around the over-restored ecclesiastical ruins and Celtic crosses and walk over to the island's deserted Atlantic beaches, it's not hard to persuade oneself that Iona's numinous tranquility owes as much to a legacy of spiritual brightness as to the softly lucent westerly light that permeates the Hebrides. Certainly, the mystical, 'God's Country' aspect of the Highlands and Islands – an ancient country littered with megalithic riddles, where every rock once doubled as a petrified soul or giant's stepping stone – accounts no less than romantic castles and picturesque scenery for Scotland's abiding allure.

The poems of Robert Burns (1759–96) make the same simple yet grand appeal to the common yearnings of humanity. Though not a Highlander, and far from being the illiterate prodigy feted by the salons of Edinburgh, Burns composed poetry of genius that rejoiced in honest sentiment. 'The wan moon sets behind the white wave, And time is setting with me, Oh!' sang the handsome, philandering tax collector, who was truly one of nature's own; or 'Had we never lov'd sae kindly – Had we never lov'd sae blindly – Never met – or never parted, We had ne'er been broken-hearted!' The result, predictable enough, was the sentimentalizing of the 'poetical ploughman' himself, whose reputation as the greatest poet of his age was not harmed by his dying young. Burns fitted the profile of romantic hero and suffered as a consequence a kind of national apotheosis. Anyone who has raised a glass to the 'Immortal Memory' at a Burns Night celebration in Ayrshire, North Queensland or Moscow knows that they have taken part in a religious ceremony. What his writings undoubtedly did was help his countrymen regain their confidence, which had been more or less trampled on by the Union with England in 1707 and the disastrous Jacobite rebellions. Here were songs that after two centuries of suppression by the gloomy doctrines of Calvinism celebrated life with its joys and sorrows; poems that reinterpreted Scotland for the benefit of all Scots; satires that proclaimed their humanity in the universal language not of radicalism but of tolerance. By restoring the self-respect of the common man so that he could see himself again as a great lover and carouser, a great fighter for freedom and democracy – 'Here's to us! Wha's like us?' – Burns created a new, assertive (some might say self-deceiving) image of Scotland that not only spread his country's fame abroad, but itself became a source of national pride and a lasting influence on the Scottish character.

'Is it not strange', wrote the rationalist philosopher David Hume in 1757, 'that, at a time when we have lost our Princes, our Parliaments, our independent Government . . . we should really be the People most distinguished for Literature in Europe?' The remark (made before Burns or Scott had been born) was nothing if not prophetic, but reflects too the extraordinary confidence of the Scottish Enlightenment (1730–1820), the great flowering of the arts and sciences and intellectual life of the country that led and influenced the Romantic movement, tempering its early exuberance, if not its later excesses, with the pragmatic common sense most often associated with the national genius. In Scottish painting, the contrasting of elegance and ruggedness that characterized the eighteenth-century sensibility of Allan Ramsay (and, in architecture,

Robert Adam) had developed by the 1820s into a fully fledged romantic style exemplified by Henry Raeburn's portraits of Highland chiefs in all their tartan glory. Landscape painting underwent a similar progression from instructive or idealized topographical views of the hitherto unknown Scottish scenery to the dramatic panoramas of wild glens loured over by gathering storms, darkling crags and ruined castles that Horatio McCulloch and others rendered as emotively as fashion demanded. With Victorian taste moving toward genre and history painting (often inspired by scenes from the novels of Sir Walter Scott), the gradual descent into sentimentality and pathos became a headlong rush and although artists like George Harvey, Edwin Landseer and the Faed brothers painted with great skill, the restraining influence of the Age of Reason upon such works as 'The Monarch of the Glen' or 'The Mitherless Bairn' was no longer perceptible.

While his romantic vision of Scotland caught the imagination of all Europe, Sir Walter Scott, born in 1771, remained always a son of the Enlightenment. His life and writings reflect a divided sensibility, loyal both to the old world and the new, recognizing the material benefits of the union with England, but drawn emotionally to the lost Stuart cause. In rewriting Scottish history not as the grim bloodstained business it was, but as the colourful dramatic pageant it might or should have been, Scott the Wizard performed a socially useful conjuring trick. He spun the tragic, not always edifying stories of William Wallace, Mary Queen of Scots, Rob Roy, Bonnie Prince Charlie and Flora Macdonald into golden legend, bequeathing his countrymen a past resplendent with heroic figures, a national pantheon, that every Scotsman could proudly identify with and safely revere. In public life, Scott's bipartisanship was revealed most tellingly in his ability to reconcile the passionate campaign he waged to recover the Scottish regalia (a pitiful reminder of Scotland's bartered identity) with the leading role he played in arranging the 1822 state visit of George IV, the Hanoverian king whom Scott introduced swathed in Royal Stuart tartan (the Wizard himself wore Campbell) to the Highland clans. Both were heavily symbolic, carefully stage-managed, unintentionally comic gestures, but partly because of Scott's

enormous personal popularity, partly because his timing was exactly right – the Romantic movement with its generous cosmopolitan spirit had finally come of age in Scotland – they succeeded beyond any reasonable expectations in healing old wounds.

If Scott's role as go-between remains controversial, it comes into clearer perspective after a visit to Abbotsford, or 'Conundrum Castle' as he christened this splendidly curious, theatrical, yet intensely personal monument to Scotland's heroic past. An unprecedented hotchpotch of architectural styles – part Scottish baronial, part gothic, part English manor house – Abbotsford cannot compare with the great eighteenth-century play castles of Inveraray and Culzean, whose gothic facades hide rich classical interiors of notable sophistication and beauty. Indeed, John Ruskin called Abbotsford 'the most incongruous pile gentlemanly modernism ever designed', but missed the point that it stands alone as a complete expression of its author's complex personality. Its toytown assemblage of mediaeval towers, crow-stepped gables and cloistered gardens was the embodiment of all Scott's extravagant dreams, his antiquarian interests and social ambitions. He suffered no inhibitions about taste, happily combining the quaint keepsakes of history with new-fangled amenities (from air-compression bells to gas lighting), modern furnishings and domestic comfort with the atmosphere of an ancient Scottish baronial keep. The balance between tradition and progress brought, perhaps unconsciously, the divisive strains of Scott's life and times peacefully together under one roof. Abbotsford can be read like a book, every fantastical detail of its construction reflecting the pleasure Scott took in creating what he described as 'this romance of a house', and others less kindly have called his finest historical novel.

The same might be said of Scotland itself, or rather the image of Scotland that Sir Walter Scott tirelessly promoted. But what began at Abbotsford: the movement to rescue and honour the memory of the clans; the fashion for touring the north generated by Scott's writings; the craze for tartan, for ruins and dramatic landscapes, for salmon fishing and deer stalking, for picturesque ghillies; the influence of Scottish 'style' on the development of nineteenth-century taste and architecture – in

Balmoral Castle

Queen Victoria, who felt an almost mystical devotion to the Highlands, called it 'this dear paradise'. A light granite neo-baronial mansion, Balmoral was built in 1853 on the site of an earlier castle by a local architect, William Smith of Aberdeen, but with considerable input from the Prince Consort. The house, which lies on a bend of the River Dee in the district of Mar, became enormously influential in the spread of the Scottish baronial 'look' both at home and abroad during the latter part of the nineteenth century. Balmoral was later blamed for the inevitable excesses of the Celtic Revival – the unrestrained use of tartan in dress and decoration, the plague of pepperpot turrets, thistle motifs and stags' antlers, and a false sentimentality about the lost Jacobite cause – but the reaction against 'Balmoralization' has been softened if not halted by Queen Elizabeth the Queen Mother's impeccable Highland pedigree and the royal family's enduring enthusiasm for their holiday home in the Highlands.

short, the Celtic Revival – only really took off after Queen Victoria and Prince Albert, newly enchanted with the northern half of their dominion, decided to build themselves an imposing schloss among the forested braes of Deeside. 'The view was so beautiful over the dear hills;' she confided to her *Journal of Our Life in the Highlands,* 'the day so fine; the whole so *gemütlich.*' In more ways than one, the great-great-niece of the Duke of Cumberland had found her way home. A holidaying monarch at Balmoral was the ultimate endorsement, the fullest possible recognition of Scotland and its place in a united kingdom; henceforth the royal mystique and the romance of the Highlands would grow together and in the public mind become inseparable.

The enthusiasm for all things Scottish soon spread from royalty to the rest of the country and excited the nostalgia of loyal Scots abroad as well as a wider interest around the world. Anyone who could claim a drop of Scottish blood draped themselves in tartan, unaware or unconcerned that most of the 'ancient clan setts' had come to light (courtesy of bogus scholarship and enterprising manufacturers) in the very recent past. Happy to follow the Prince Consort's example, English industrialists bought up mortgaged highland estates and built on them faux baronial strengths whose pinnacled turrets and draughty halls bristled with stags' antlers and knobbly furniture upholstered in tweed and yet more tartan. There, after the virile fashion set by Balmoral, they devoted the summer months to healthy outdoor pursuits: hunting wild game, picnicing in the heather, watching local worthies perform at Highland gatherings and learning to dance reels and strathspeys in the damp, hooting moonlight. What soon became known as the Scottish season was naturally encouraged by impoverished Highland lairds, who were more than happy to lease their ancestral salmon rivers and grouse moors to (as they saw them) gullible customers from the south, ensuring their own survival by turning a distinctly Germanic tradition of ritualized slaughter and romantic posturing in the wild into an exclusive, still very much sought after Highland experience.

Although among the first to bow to royal influence and 'Balmoralize' their houses, the old Scottish families were fortunately seldom rich

The 'Balmoral' Room

As an example of how tempting it must have been to the Victorians to take the tartan theme to its limits, the Fine Art Society in Edinburgh created a 'Balmoral' room for the Edinburgh Festival in 1986, complete with Lindsay tartan walls and Royal Stuart tented ceiling.

Kati and Jane Dudgeon of Aberfeldy

At every Highland games, the dancing competitions are among the most popular events. These stylized displays of high leaps and nimble-footedness, which children growing up in the Highlands are encouraged to learn, bear scant resemblance to the dances the Romans noted the ancient Caledonians performed, hurling themselves wildly around their unsheathed swords, stuck points upwards in the ground. Much has been written about the symbolic significance of reels, linking their circular patterns with ritual worship of the sun, fertility, even the devil. In historic times, Mary Queen of Scots and her French entourage helped tidy up some of the Scottish folk dances performed at court, and introduced others. The Highland regiments also played an important role in preserving traditional reels and strathspeys, and continue to do so.

enough to do so. As a result, an impressive list of lesser-known historic buildings came through the Victorian period unscathed. Not that all neo-baronial architecture in Scotland was a disaster: the work of Sir Charles Barry at Dunrobin Castle, for instance, achieves a dizzying ersatz splendour. The Victorians also built manses, shooting lodges, farms and small laird's houses that respected local styles and traditions. But, in their attempts to elevate the vernacular, they too often ignored what is most characteristic about Scotland's architecture: simple, robust proportions, restrained use of ornament and the impression early Scottish houses give of rising naturally out of the landscape. Whether a humble crofter's cottage, doughty castle or flamboyant Jacobean towerhouse, the need to site buildings defensively or for shelter, the use of sympathetic local materials, produced the pleasing effect of houses sensibly adapted to a demanding environment. The romantic aspect of such buildings – their often turbulent history, the remoteness that protected them from change, the sturdy witness they bear to the frailty of human existence – was more sensitively interpreted by the Edwardian architects, Sir Robert Lorimer and Charles Rennie Mackintosh, who recognized the stern aesthetic of necessity and adversity in Scotland's architectural tradition and in their different ways assimilated it into their work. But the spurious baronial image that Balmoral and the Victorians had converted into an easily recognizable, international style had by the end of the nineteenth century become another powerful stereotype of 'Scottishness' – that cohesive romantic identity that Ossian, Burns and Scott wrapped around Scotland, and Scotland has never been able or willing to shed.

When I was growing up in Argyll, thirty-odd years ago, it seemed as natural as it was necessary (in order to better distinguish the 'real' Highlands) to make fun of institutionalized Scottish romanticism. An untroubled fan of Robert Louis Stevenson and John Buchan, whose stirring adventures set in the Highlands passed muster because they seemed to me almost subversively authentic, I found Scott unreadable, mocked at pictures of roaring stags and 'mitherless bairns' and regarded what might be called the Balmoral factor – epitomized by newscasts of the royal princes mucking about on Deeside in neatly pressed kilts and

Edinburgh, from Calton Hill

It's not every citizen of Glasgow who will speak well of Scotland's capital. The poet Alexander Smith does and, in my view, captures perfectly the spirit of this incomparable city.

'Living in Edinburgh there abides, above all things, a sense of its beauty. Hill, crag, castle, rock, blue stretch of sea, the picturesque ridge of the Old Town, the squares and terraces of the New – these things once seen are not to be forgotten . . . Across the ravine Time has piled up the Old Town, ridge on ridge, grey as a rocky coast washed and worn by the foam of centuries; peaked and jagged by gable and roof; windowed from basement to cope; the whole surmounted by St Giles's airy crown. The New is there looking at the Old. Two Times are brought face to face, and are yet separated by a thousand years. Wonderful on winter nights, when the gully is filled with darkness, and out of it rises, against the sombre blue and frosty stars, that mass and bulwark of gloom, pierced and quivering with innumerable lights. There is nothing in Europe to match that, I think.'

ALEXANDER SMITH (1830–67)

polished brogues – as a faintly embarrassing irrelevance. Now I would find it harder to deny that the Victorians in some ways helped preserve the traditions of the Scottish countryside; or that the royal family with its strengthened Highland connection has consistently boosted the Scots' confidence in their mythic identity. Harder, too, to separate the feelings I share with most Highlanders – the reflexes of ancestral pride, the communal sense of belonging, the irrational love of a barren, rain-sodden country, a born weakness for the sound of the pipes across water – from the romantic outlook that over two centuries has become engrained in our history and national character.

It's not just that time tends to blur such distinctions. Or that reaction against what many see as a damagingly false picture of Scotland, ranging from wry debunking to shrill protest, has been so ineffectual: our resistance crumbling spectacularly before the spending power of the millions of visitors who come north every year in search of the same ineffable spirit of romance that lured the first tourists over the border. Sir Walter Scott may have founded the nation's most profitable enterprise, but he cannot be held responsible (any more than Landseer or Queen Victoria can) for its having spawned the kilted trolls, squeaky highland cows and Royal Stuart toilet roll covers that fill gift shop shelves from Gretna to Tongue. Unjustly reviled by the poet Edwin Muir as 'a sham bard of a sham nation', the Wizard of the North no doubt exploited Celtic pride and sentimentality and partialness to storytelling; succeeded, what's more, in selling the heady brew to the sober, industrious Lowlander; but he never oversentimentalized Scotland's past and, in a country as divided by history, custom and language as by its discouraging geography, he created through the unifying power of literature something like national concord. It is surely revealing that Edinburgh is dominated (as no other capital city) by a monument to a writer: Scott's rocket-ship gothic shrine, the largest and tallest literary memorial in the world, having been erected by a nation grateful to the romantic imagination that made legends of its memories, and reinvented a Scotland that would always be Scotland.

Overleaf

Bridgeview Cottage, Balnaguard

The tendency has been to consign the old black ranges, once so common in Scottish houses, to the scrapheap. They are in fact an efficient and economical way of keeping the heart of a house warm, heating hot water (if fitted with a back-boiler), and cooking – all with the minimum of fuss and for the same bucket of coal, peat or pile of sticks. I have one myself and would not part with it for anything.

ROMANTIC SCOTLAND

In the highlands, in the country places,
Where the old plain men have rosy faces,
And the young fair maidens
Quiet eyes;
Where essential silence cheers and blesses,
And for ever in the hill-recesses
Her more lovely music
Broods and dies.

O to mount again where erst I haunted;
Where the old red hills are bird-enchanted,
And the low green meadows
Bright with sward;
And when even dies, the million-tinted,
And the night has come, and planets glinted,
Lo, the valley hollow
Lamp-bestarred.

O to dream, O to awake and wander
There, and with delight to take and render,
Through the trance of silence,
Quiet breath;
Lo! for there, among the flowers and grasses,
Only the mightier movement sounds and passes;
Only winds and rivers,
Life and death.

ROBERT LOUIS STEVENSON
'In the Highlands'

Hermitage Castle

'All the gentlemen's houses are strong castles, they being so treacherous to one another, that they are forced to defend themselves in strongholds', wrote Thomas Kirke as late as 1679. The Scots, indeed, carried on living behind battlements and fighting each other longer than anyone else in Europe, with the possible exception of Albania. Few 'houses' are more impressive than Hermitage, 'the strength of Liddesdale', with its air of massive impregnability. A testimony to the troubled centuries of conflict on the Border between Scotland and England, Hermitage changed hands at irregular intervals, and violently, throughout the Middle Ages. It is known for its romantic association with Mary Queen of Scots, who in 1566 galloped from Jedburgh to visit the wounded Bothwell at Hermitage.

Berwick-upon-Tweed

On the north bank of the River Tweed, one of Scotland's great salmon rivers, Berwick is a fortified town of famously divided loyalties. Politically part of Northumberland, England, but also a Scottish royal burgh, the town changed hands no less than thirteen times during the Scottish Wars of Independence (from the twelfth to sixteenth centuries) before becoming independent itself of both countries. Berwick is technically still at war with Russia having failed to sign the peace treaty after the Crimean War. Its long history of feuds and battles between the Scots and English is representative of the conflicts that raged through the Border country to the west known as the Debatable Land.

Manderston

An extraordinarily opulent
Edwardian country house near
Duns in Berwickshire, Manderston
was built to impress. Not just the
world, but one man in particular.
Sir James Miller, who inherited
a huge fortune from his father,
Sir William Miller of Leith in
Edinburgh, married into the
Curzon family of Kedleston Hall
in Derbyshire. Hoping to outdo his
famous brother-in-law, George
Curzon, who became 1st Marquess
of Kedleston and Viceroy of India,
Sir James spared no expense in
making Manderston a palace of
ease and luxury. The staircase is a
copy of one at the Petit Trianon at
Versailles. But here, below stairs,
are the fifty-six bells, each with a
different tone, that hang outside
what once was the housekeeper's
room.

Thirlestane Castle

On the morning of 21 September 1745, Prince Charles Edward's army of Highlanders won a quick and decisive victory over the government forces led by Sir John Cope at Prestonpans. Cope fled to England, the first to bear the news of his own defeat. The dawn rout is celebrated in the Jacobite song, 'Hey Johnny Cope, are ye waulking yet?' After what turned out to be the highpoint of the Jacobites' ill-fated campaign, Prince Charlie spent the night in this room at Thirlestane Castle, the seat of the earls of Lauderdale near Lauder in Berwickshire. The old castle was built in 1590, but greatly extended in the Restoration style by one of Scotland's greatest architects, Sir William Bruce. The splendid plasterwork ceilings designed by Robert Mylne and carried out by Dutch craftsmen are generally considered to be among the finest in Scotland.

Sheep Enclosure, Cheviot Hills

Enormously influential in his lifetime as a prophet, social critic and inspirer of self-educated men, Thomas Carlyle remained deeply attached to the Border country where he grew up. The picture of pastoral bliss he paints here may be sentimentalized, but something like it still can be found among the Cheviots.

'We walked up Meggat Water to beyond the sources, emerged into Yarrow not far above St Mary's Loch; a charming secluded shepherd country with excellent shepherd population . . . lodged with shepherds who had clean solid cottages; wholesome eggs, milk, oatbread, porridge, clean blankets to their beds, and a great deal of human sense and unadul-terated natural politeness. Canty, shrewd, and witty fellows, when you set them talking; knew from their hilltops every bit of country between Forth and Solway, and all the shepherd inhabitants within fifty miles, being a kind of confraternity of shepherds from father to son. No sort of peasant labourers I have ever come across seemed to me so happily situated, morally and physically well-developed, and deserving to be happy, as those shepherds of the Cheviots.'

THOMAS CARLYLE (1795-1881)

Traquair House

Traquair is said to be the oldest inhabited house in Scotland. It was a royal hunting lodge when Alexander I rode down wolves in nearby Ettrick forest and since then has been visited by twenty-six Scottish and English monarchs. Much added to over the centuries but chiefly built in the reign of Charles I, with its round turrets and steep roofs Traquair has the look of a French chateau. The place fairly reeks of romance. Mary Queen of Scots and Darnley were guests here in 1566 and some of her relics are kept in the house. Bonnie Prince Charlie was another visitor to Traquair in 1745. According to a popular story – encouraged, if not started, by Sir Walter Scott – the following year the famous Bear Gates to the main Avenue were ordered shut by the Earl of Traquair, not to be opened until a Stuart again sat on the throne.

Abbotsford

Sir Walter Scott once described Abbotsford, the neo-baronial mansion he built himself near Melrose on the banks of the Tweed, as a 'romance of a house'. An uninhibited mixture of architectural styles, every detail of its construction was informed by the author's extravagant antiquarian interests. The porch, for example, was modelled on the one at Linlithgow Palace; the screen wall enclosing the court was copied from the cloisters at Melrose Abbey; the very walls of Abbotsford were embedded with fragments and keepsakes of Scotland's history.

The Armoury (*left*) contains such significant weapons as Rob Roy's dirk and gun, Claverhouse's pistol and Montrose's sword. Also on display are drawings and paintings of Scott's family and his favourite pets, dog 'Ginger', and cat 'Hinse of Hinsefeldt', as well as a strange likeness of the head of Mary Queen of Scots made by Amyas Cawood the day after she lost it on the scaffold. The contemporary portrait above the fireplace is of James IV of Scotland.

The Forth Bridge

The rail bridge across the Firth of Forth, built between 1883 and 1890 by Sir John Fowler, was considered one of the great engineering feats of the day. The bridge is just over a mile long and straddles the Forth in four mighty spans, its railway track running 157 feet above the water. The painted surface represents 135 acres. Below the bridge, the tiny island of Inchgarvie has a fifteenth-century fort on it which held out against Cromwell in 1650 and was rebuilt to warn off the American privateer, John Paul Jones, in 1779.

Culross

One of the best examples of a small sixteenth- to seventeenth-century Scottish town, Culross owes its survival as an unspoilt whole both to its own history and to the efforts of the National Trust for Scotland. In its heyday Culross enjoyed a thriving trade in salt and coal and had overseas contacts with the Baltic and the Low Countries. When its chief enterprises failed, the town declined and became a backwater overlooked by the industrial developments of the nineteenth century. For the past sixty years, the NTS has been engaged in restoring the old houses of the town; the cobbled streets, crow-stepped gables and red pantiled roofs appearing virtually unchanged. One of the most interesting buildings to be restored and opened to visitors is 'The Palace', the quite modest home of Sir George Bruce, which gives a fascinating picture of Scottish life in the late sixteenth and early seventeenth centuries.

Stirling Castle

Strategically sited on top of an extinct volcano rising from the valley of the Forth, Stirling Castle has been witness to some key moments in Scottish history. Two great battles associated with the struggle for independence were fought here or close by. The first, in 1297, was the Battle of Stirling Bridge, where Sir William Wallace trapped and routed an English army. Then, in 1314, it was Edward II's attempt to relieve his beleaguered governor in the castle that led to his defeat by Robert the Bruce at Bannockburn. The present building dates mostly from the fifteenth century and includes a very beautiful Renaissance great hall. The castle is now the headquarters of the Argyll and Sutherland Highlanders.

Gleneagles

One of the most famous golfing resorts in the world, Gleneagles Hotel, looks south to the Ochil Hills. The view here is down the glen from Gleneagles House, which was built in 1624 replacing an ancient moated castle; it has been home to the Haldane family for at least 800 years. The nearby St Mungo's chapel (twelfth-century) contains many Haldane memorials. The name Glen Eagles, incidentally, has nothing to do with birds or golf scores, but derives from 'eaglais', meaning 'church'.

Drummond Castle

An intimate corner of the grandest parterre in Scotland, which was first laid out on a series of natural terraces in 1630 and redesigned in the 1820s. On the whole the Scottish landscape does not lend itself to formal gardens, but against the backdrop of Perthshire farmland, the symmetry and order of Drummond comes as a pleasing surprise at the end of a mile long avenue. The seat of the Earl of Ancaster, the castle was built in 1491 by John, Lord Drummond, from whom he is descended in the female line. The Drummonds were staunch Jacobites and in 1745 the castle was partly demolished by the family to prevent its occupation by Hanoverian troops.

Anstruther

Known locally as 'Ainster', the Royal Burghs of Anstruther Easter and Anstruther Wester stand either side of the harbour to this old-fashioned seaport and fishing village, which lies on the north shore of the Firth of Forth. The houses with their pantile roofs and 'Dutch' tympan gables are typical of east Fife. The church in Anstruther Easter was built in 1634 and honours a native son, Dr Thomas Chalmers (1780-1840), First Moderator of the Assembly of the Free Church of Scotland and a tireless worker among the Glasgow poor. The manse dates from 1590 and is said to be the oldest continuously occupied manse in Scotland. Until the herring shoals disappeared after the Second World War, Ainster was known for its prodigious catches of 'the silver darlings'. Fishing is still part of the life of the community, but has been gradually superseded by tourism.

Crail

The most easterly port of Fife, this picturesque fishing town lies on the rocky coast that faces Dunbar across the Firth of Forth. A royal burgh since 1310, its charter includes the unusual privilege of allowing trading on the sabbath. This did not prevent mercantile setbacks in the seventeenth century, which coupled with an outbreak of plague reduced Crail's importance as a trading and fishing port. In the eighteenth century, its old stone houses that line the steep streets leading to the harbour became the haunt of smugglers. The town now has a reputation as a haven for artists.

St Andrews

The ruin of what was once the largest church in Scotland rises gauntly by the edge of the North Sea. The building of the cathedral at St Andrews was begun by Bishop Arnold in 1161 and completed in 1318. While it withstood onslaughts of fire and flood during the Middle Ages, the cathedral did not survive the damage inflicted on it by the zeal of the Reformation. In 1559, John Knox preached a violent sermon against idolatry, which was taken to heart by the townspeople of St Andrews who reduced the building to a shell and over the next couple of centuries used the rubble as a supply of building materials. Dr Johnson, prowling morosely among the ruins, was asked where John Knox was buried, to which he replied: 'I hope in the highway! I have been looking at his reformation.'

Earlshall Castle

A 'Z-plan' tower house, built for the Bruce family in the late sixteenth century, Earlshall, near Leuchars in Fife, was restored by the Edwardian architect, Sir Robert Lorimer. It was his first and some consider his best work of restoration. The courtyard garden created by Lorimer is famous for the topiary chessmen he transplanted from a derelict Edinburgh garden in 1894 and laid out in the shape of a saltire.

The long gallery at Earlshall, decorated in grisaille with a mixture of heraldry, symbolic figures and pithy epithets, was restored and partly repainted under Lorimer's careful instructions. A peculiarly Scottish phenomenon – domestic painted ceilings are rarely found in England – painted decoration in Scotland dates roughly from 1570 to 1650. A mediaeval tradition, it was originally associated only with religious buildings. When the Reformation brought the decoration of churches to an abrupt halt in 1560, it left the craftsmen free to continue applying their art in the houses of nobles and merchants. Some of the best known examples can be found at Crathes, Stobhall and Pinkie House.

Earlshall Castle

The claymore (from the Gaelic 'claidheamh-mor', literally 'great sword') was a Highland version of the European double-handed sword. As terrible in battle as it was unwieldy, it was replaced during the sixteenth century by the lighter basket-hilted broad-sword which became the Highlander's weapon of choice.

Like a tempest down the ridges
Swept the hurricane of steel
Rose the slogan of Macdonald –
Flashed the broadsword of Lochiel!
Vainly sped the withering volley
'Mongst the foremost of our band –
On we poured until we met them,
Foot to foot, and hand to hand.
Horse and man went down like drift-wood
When the floods are black at Yule,
And their carcases are whirling
In the Garry's deepest pool.
Horse and man went down before us –
Living foe there tarried none
On the field at Killiekrankie,
When the stubborn fight was done!

From 'The Battle of Killiekrankie'
by W.E. AYTOUN (1813-65)

Kinnaird Estate

Jim Tritton and Donny Calder, wearing Kinnaird estate tweed, survey the grouse moor. Little Loch Skiach is in the distance.

Glamis Castle

A brooding presence even on a sunny day, with its dark clusters of corbelled turrets and battlemented parapets overlooking Dean Water in the Vale of Strathmore, Glamis Castle was mostly rebuilt in the seventeenth century. But the castle, known for its literary association with Shakespeare's *Macbeth*, contains fragments of a much older building and is thought to have been a royal residence in the eleventh century. The ancestral seat of the earls of Strathmore, and childhood home of Queen Elizabeth the Queen Mother, Glamis bristles with historical incident: Malcolm II may have died or been murdered here in 1034; a Lady Glamis was burnt for witchcraft in 1537; the Old Pretender held court at Glamis in 1715; the last court jester earned his keep hamming it up in Duncan's Hall – nor is there any shortage of revenants. It has often been said of Glamis that it is the most haunted house in Scotland.

Blair Castle

The last castle in Britain to be besieged (in 1746, prior to the Battle of Culloden), Blair in Atholl, Perthshire, is the seat of the Murray family, who have been earls and dukes of Atholl since the sixteenth century. The oldest part of the castle was built in 1269; it was extensively renovated in the eighteenth century, then re-baronialized by the Victorian architect David Bryce, who restored the mediaeval-style turrets and crow-stepped gables. Parts of Blair are open to the public, and as a centre for various activities from piping competitions to horse trials it attracts large numbers of visitors. The Duke of Atholl is the only British subject permitted to retain a standing army – the Atholl Highlanders – a privilege granted by Queen Victoria after she visited Blair in 1844, still in the first flush of her love affair with the Highlands.

The Royal Scotsman

In 1985 the Great Scottish and Western Railway Company began operation of a luxury train service on little used railway lines through the Highlands. Since then the Royal Scotsman, which carries a maximum of thirty-two passengers, has earned the reputation of achieving the highest standards of comfort and cuisine on any train service anywhere in the world. On part of its route, the refitted Pullman stock carriages of the Royal Scotsman are drawn by a steam locomotive from the London Midland & Scottish. It is seen here crossing the Glenfinnan Viaduct en route for the west coast fishing port of Mallaig.

Dunkeld

On the Perth to Inverness stretch of the old Highland railway, this mechanically operated signal box at Dunkeld (one of the remaining few) recalls the days when travel by train in and to Scotland had a romance all its own – days that are not altogether gone. The age of steam may have been more appealing, but taking the sleeper train from London to the north, leaving behind the squalor of Euston at midnight and waking up among the rugged Highland hills and glens, still retains a Buchanesque flavour of adventure. In the West Highland line, which runs from Glasgow to Fort William, crossing the gloriously wild desert of Rannoch Moor, Scotland can boast the most scenic and romantic railway in the world.

The River Tay

The Tay is one of Scotland's best-known salmon rivers. With its huge catchment area and many tributaries, among them the Tummel, the Ericht and the Lyon, it discharges into the sea at Perth the greatest body of water of any river in Britain. Broad and slow-moving (at least compared to the spate rivers of the north-west), the Tay challenges the fly fisherman's casting abilities and many beats have to be fished from a boat. The Tay also holds the unbeaten record for the heaviest salmon ever caught in Britain, a 67lb fish taken on the Glendelvine beat in 1926 by a young girl. Some 10,000 salmon are caught on the rod in these waters every season, although in recent years pollution, netting at sea and fish farming have taken their toll on salmon catches in rivers and lochs all over Scotland.

The River Dee

An iron suspension bridge crosses the Dee downriver from Balmoral. It was built largely for the convenience of salmon fishermen in 1924. The Dee, particularly the area bound by Ballater and Braemar, has come to be associated with the royal family: hence 'Royal Deeside'. The river's upper reaches west of Braemar are wilder and faster flowing; it was in the Linn of Dee, a rocky ravine near Inverey, that Lord Byron came close to losing his life.

Invercauld House

In the courtyard of Invercauld House, Captain Alwyne Farquharson of Invercauld (*centre left*) lines up with keepers and loaders before the day's shoot. Not far from where the shooting party breaks for lunch stands Cairn na Cuimhne (Cairn of Remembrance), the rallying place of the Farquharsons. When the clan gathered here before a battle, each fighting man brought and left a stone; on returning, every man took back a stone from the pile; the number of stones left lying on the ground marked the clan's loss. It was from Invercauld, the ancient seat of the Farquharsons, that the Earl of Mar called out the clans for the 1715 Rising.

Braemar Castle

Under the guise of a hunting party, the Earl of Mar and a band of loyal Jacobites gathered at Braemar on 26 August 1715. Here they made the fateful decision to raise the standard for James VIII, which resulted in the half-hearted '15 rebellion, which fizzled out within the year at the Battle of Sheriffmuir. Braemar Castle, built by the Earl of Mar in 1628, burned by the Farquharsons sixty years later, was garrisoned by English troops both after the '15 and the '45 to control the still turbulent Highlands. The battlements, crenellations and star-shaped ramparts, loopholed for muskets, date from the last occupation. An interesting example of a Hanoverian fort, as architecture Braemar Castle gives an incongruous impression. A caber's toss from Balmoral, the famous Braemar Gathering takes place in the nearby village every September. First attended by Queen Victoria in 1848, the gathering remains a firm fixture on the royal family's calendar.

Braemar

Victorian porches added to buildings in the Highlands were not meant to be functional, but provided an opportunity for inventiveness and decorative exuberance that reflected the romantic spirit of the age. Decorative features commonly included finials, strutting, and, as here, pillars made from fir tree trunks with the stumps of branches left protruding to give a rustic effect. It was to a cottage in Braemar, similar to this one, that Robert Louis Stevenson came for a holiday in 1880 and, because it rained most of the time, wrote a story based on an imaginary map for his bored stepson, Lloyd Osbourne, and called it 'The Sea Cook or Treasure Island'.

Corgarff Castle

A stark and lonely tower high in the Grampian hills, Corgarff has commanded the road between Ballater and Tomintoul since 1537. The tower has seen its share of cruel, bloody deeds. It was badly damaged in 1571, when, after being besieged by a party of Gordons and bravely defended by the wife of the absent owner, Alexander Forbes, Corgarff was set on fire. Margaret Forbes with her children and servants 'to a total of twenty-seven' perished in the flames. In 1645 Montrose spent a month here before the Battle of Alford and in 1715 the Earl of Mar camped at Corgarff before raising the Jacobite standard at Braemar. During the '45 the castle was turned into a fortified barracks by the Hanoverian forces, who added the unusual star-shaped curtain wall in 1748, by which time Corgarff was being used as a centre for hunting down Jacobite fugitives.

Crathes Castle

The interior of Crathes (1553-94), one of the most striking and best preserved Aberdeenshire tower houses, is famous for its painted ceilings, which were discovered under a covering of lath and plaster in 1877. Shown here is a segment of the ceiling decoration in the Room of the Nine Nobles (c.1600), which depicts three pagan, three Old Testament and three Christian figures, and in verse asks of the visitor to decide which of these nobles was the most valiant.

The gardens at Crathes were formally laid out in the eighteenth century, enclosed by walls and subdivided by massive yew hedges that date from 1702. Covering an area of six acres, the garden or series of garden rooms was principally created in the 1920s by Sir James Burnett, whose knowledge of trees and shrubs was complemented by his wife's flair for colour and design. Their partnership produced one of Scotland's great gardens, which has been run by the National Trust since 1951 without any loss to its charm or individuality.

Craigievar Castle

Few would contest that Craigievar Castle in Aberdeenshire is the apotheosis of the Jacobean tower house, a style of building native to Scotland that represents the most characteristic, influential and perhaps finest achievement of Scottish architecture. A family mansion in the martial style, rather than a defensive structure, Craigievar was built between 1600 and 1626 by William Forbes, a successful Aberdeen merchant better known (for having made his fortune in Baltic trading) as 'Danzig Willie'. A simple, 'L-plan' tower rising seven storeys straight from the ground to a glorious crown of corbelled turrets, bartizans and balustrades, angle roofs and crow-stepped gables, it has remained virtually untouched over the centuries. The interior, equally intact, boasts in its great hall one of the finest Renaissance plaster ceilings in the country. Over the cavernous fireplace are carved the Forbes family's coat of arms and the appropriate warning: 'Doe not vaiken sleiping dogs'.

Loanhead Stone Circle

In the neolithic heartland of
north-eastern Scotland, the third
millennium BC saw the development of a unique and mysterious
type of megalithic monument
known as the recumbent stone
circle or circle of the moon. The
circles, usually found on the
crests of hills or terraces with
southerly views, often contain,
as in the case of Loanhead, low
burial mounds called ring cairns,
but these were almost certainly
added later to existing sites. The
primary function of the stone
circle centred on the massive
recumbent slab and its flanking
pillars, which are arranged to
frame the rising or setting of
the moon in the southern sky.
Although still the subject of
debate, they were probably used
to make lunar observations that
would have helped the primitive
farming communities that built
the circles define seasonal
changes and carry out various
ritual ceremonies.

The Livet Water

The picturesque remains of an old bridge span the Livet Water near Bridgend in Banffshire. The famous Glenlivet distillery was founded in 1824, one of the five in the area that survived the Distillery Act which closed down some 200 illicit stills. A pure malt whisky, 'Glenlivet' used to be made from barley grown locally, but the demand for the product is such that most of the grain now has to be imported from England. At the head of the glen there are the ruins of a Catholic seminary founded in 1717, where young men were trained in secret for the priesthood. It was discovered and destroyed by the Hanoverian forces after their victory over the Jacobites at Culloden.

Dusk in the Grampians

Harp of the North, farewell! The hills grow dark,
On purple peaks a deeper shade descending;
In twilight copse the glow-worm lights her spark,
The deer, half seen, are to the covert wending.
Resume thy wizard elm! the fountain lending,
And the wild breeze, thy wilder minstrelsy;
Thy numbers sweet with nature's vespers blending,
With distant echo from the fold and lea,
And herd-boy's evening pipe and hum of housing bee.

SIR WALTER SCOTT (1771-1832)
The Lady of the Lake

Cooperage at Dufftown

Rome was built on seven hills;
Dufftown stands on seven stills.

Or so runs the popular jingle that
celebrates Dufftown's claim to be
the capital of Scotland's malt-
distilling industry. The town was
founded in 1817 by James Duff,
4th Earl of Fife, to create local
employment after the Napoleonic
wars. The appetizing smell of
roasting malt fills the air and
comes from the multitude of
distilleries in and around
Dufftown, which lies near the
junction of the River Fiddich and
Dullan Water. The famous
Glenfiddich and Balvenie
distilleries are among others
open to visitors on the Speyside
'whisky trail'.

Kinveachy Lodge

All set for a day on the hill, Jim Gillies and Frank Law stand below Kinveachy Lodge near Boat of Garten. Stalking has long been considered a noble sport in Scotland, and with good reason. Physically demanding, it can involve walking for perhaps twenty miles over rugged terrain, crawling through peat-bogs and scrambling up icy water courses. The pleasure lies in the stalk itself, the thrill of the chase, as much as the kill. Of all blood sports, stalking brings the closest involvement with the natural world and encourages a feeling of kinship with the wilderness that can produce moments of sheer exhilaration. Built for the Earl of Seafield in the nineteenth century, when the passion for deer stalking in the Highlands reached its climax, Kinveachy Lodge is now run by the Seafield family on a commercial basis.

Davidston House

A seventeenth-century 'bonnet laird's' fortified farmhouse in the Banffshire uplands, Davidston was the residence of the Gordon-Duffs until the family built themselves a neo-baronial castle at nearby Drummuir in Victorian times. The house is full of stories, one concerning an admiral's wife who caught scarlet fever and was shut up in a wing where, apart from being fed scraps of food shoved under the door, she was left to die. A former resident describes Davidston as being a 'dramatic but rather cold house, and not only because it's 750 feet up . . . there were certain bits you definitely didn't go into at night.' One friend had a problem with the kitchen (the cozy living end of the kitchen is pictured *right*), often finding herself with an unbidden companion when she had every reason to think she was enjoying the warmth of the fire alone.

Cawdor Castle

In the wooded hills of Nairnshire, celebrated for its connection with *Macbeth* (Thane of Cawdor was a title promised to Macbeth by the witches), the castle was in fact built in the fourteenth century long after the period in which Shakespeare set his play. In the vault at Cawdor, a hawthorn tree of supposedly great antiquity grows out of the flagstoned floor. As the story goes, one of the early thanes, trying to decide where to locate his new castle, dreamt that he should tie a coffer of gold to the back of a donkey and build his keep wherever the wandering donkey first stopped for a rest. He followed the advice he had received in his sleep. The donkey stopped in the shade of a hawthorn tree, around which Cawdor Castle was duly built.

Culloden Forest

It was here, on 16 April 1746,
a bitterly cold day and snowing,
that Bonnie Prince Charlie
and his ragged Highland army,
exhausted and hungry after
an all-night march, went into
battle against a fresh, disciplined
Government force more than
twice their number.

'The whole was over in about
twenty-five minutes. The Duke's
artillery [Duke of Cumberland,
commanding the Hanoverian
forces] kept still playing though
not a soul upon the field. His
army was kept together all but
the horse. The great pursuit was
on the road towards Inverness.
Of towards 6000 men, which the
Prince's army [Bonnie Prince
Charlie and the Highlanders] at
this period consisted of, about
1000 were asleep in Culloden
parks, who knew nothing of the
action till awaked by the noise of
the cannon. These in general
tried to save themselves by
taking the road towards
Inverness; and most of them fell
a sacrifice to the victors, for this
road was in general strewed with
dead bodies. The Prince at this
moment had his cheeks bedewed
with tears; what must not his
feelings have suffered.'

SIR ROBERT STRANGE,
eye-witness to the Battle of
Culloden, 1746

**Doocots at
Culloden House** (*left*)
and Glamis Castle (*right*)

Until the introduction of turnips
and swedes in the eighteenth
century, allowing livestock to be
kept throughout the year, pigeons
provided the only source of fresh
meat during the long Scottish
winters. Living larders where
pigeons were kept and fattened
for meat, doocots (dovecotes)
now number about 700 in
Scotland. In the Highlands, most
surviving doocots are found on
great estates, reflecting their
former importance as status
symbols, offering a rare chance
for displaying architectural
inventiveness. They were built
in all shapes and sizes: round,
square, octagonal; styled like
towers, lecterns, beehives;
decorated with pinnacles, finials
and crow-stepped gables. There
is a superstition in Scotland that
it's unlucky to pull down a
doocot, which may be a reason
for so many of these picturesque
monuments having survived.

Glen Urquhart

Until the 1920s, Glen Urquhart above Loch Ness was a remote valley cut off from the outside world and, accordingly, full of legends. Famed for its Gaelic, which was said to be the purest in Scotland, it also had the reputation, in spite of its great beauty, for being a place where the power of evil was constantly felt, boasting three kinds of devil – the black, the speckled and the white – and any number of witches, all of 'black' persuasion. In the ruined Castle Urquhart, which stands at the foot of the glen on the shores of Loch Ness, there are two hidden vaults, one of which is said to contain treasure, the other, the plague, kept magically bottled there until it shall be needed again.

Castle Stuart

An early seventeenth-century tower house, probably built by an earl of Murray, Castle Stuart lies north-east of Inverness close to the Moray Firth. It represents a period of transition in castle building as the domestic tower gradually evolved from fortress to mansion house, becoming less grim, more livable and, architecturally, more elaborate, while still retaining the distinguished aspect of a castle. Scotland's history continued in its turbulent course throughout the seventeenth and first half of the eighteenth century, but the need for physical strength in a building declined, and the lairds and lesser nobles in their embattled towers were becoming more interested in comfort and convenience than defence and martial ambition.

The River Beauly

The name of the river and the town that lies on its banks comes from the French beau lieu, and indeed it is a 'beautiful place'. The Beauly runs through country long associated with the Frasers, originally a Norman family who founded one of the great Highland clans. Dounie Castle, the seat of Mac Shimi, 'Son of Simon', as the Frasers of Lovat call their chiefs, was destroyed by the Duke of Cumberland after the '45. The present Beaufort Castle was built on the same site overlooking the river about 1880. Simon Fraser, 11th Lord Lovat, a wily politician and a much admired figure in the Highlands, was beheaded as a Jacobite in 1747 for his part in the Rising, the last peer of the realm to be executed for high treason. On his way to the scaffold, a cockney woman in the crowd shouted at him: 'You'll soon get that nasty head of yours chopped off, you ugly old Scotch dog!' To which the eighty-year-old Lovat, whom I'm proud to be able to call my ancestor, replied calmly: 'I believe I shall, you ugly old English bitch.'

Highland Cow

No doubt because this is a cold, northern country, there's a tendency to associate and emblematize Scotland with hairiness – hairy tweeds and sweaters, hairy chins and knees, hairy sporrans, hairy little dogs, hairy thistles and, most familiar of all, the dearly bedraggled hairiness of Highland cattle. Through no fault of their own these hardy, shaggy-headed beasts, who look like a sporting cross between a Texas longhorn and a yak but in fact are carefully bred in valuable pedigree herds, have become the winningest performers in the picture postcard drama of the Highland landscape.

Strathpeffer

The discovery of mineral springs in the eighteenth century attracted the first visitors to Strathpeffer. By the end of the Victorian era the town had become a popular spa and resort with a pavilion, rheumatic hospital and five sulphur and chalybeate wells of varying strengths. For a time it was fashionable enough to attract European royalty. Although the grand pump room has been dismantled, Strathpeffer, with its wide streets, gardens, Victorian houses and hotels, retains its period charm and an atmosphere somewhat reminiscent of an Indian hill station. In 1960, a small pump room was reopened and the waters of the spa can still be taken in what according to legend was a favourite bathing place of the Devil.

The Falls of Rogie

A few miles north-west of Strathpeffer, the Rogie Falls on the River Blackwater have become a well-known 'beauty spot', where visitors come to watch wild salmon leap. On the way to their spawning grounds in the gravelly reaches at the top of a river, salmon can jump eleven feet or more to get up a waterfall, taking off from the pool below at a speed of twenty miles per hour, the thrust generated by the action of their powerful tails.

Cromarty East

This church in Cromarty, on the eastern tip of the Black Isle, is a typical Scottish kirk of the eighteenth century. The interior with its three lofts (one for the laird; one for the schoolmaster and his pupils; and a third for anyone who wished to pay for the privilege and comfort) and all its pews orientated to face the pulpit – as opposed to the pre-Reformation habit of focusing the congregation's attention on the altar – remains unchanged and is of particular charm and interest. The kirk was often attended by Hugh Miller (1802-56), a self-educated stonemason born in Cromarty, who became a famous geologist, writer and theologian.

The Black Isle, looking north-west to Ben Wyvis

The Black Isle is not an island but a broad fertile peninsula that juts out between the Beauly and Moray firths and the Firth of Cromarty. Some say it owes its name to the fact that it enjoys a mild climate and is rarely covered by snow; others that 'Black Isle' derives from the Gaelic Eilean Dubh, which itself is a corruption of Eilean Dubhthaich – St Duthac's Isle. St Duthac, a missionary, was active in the area at the turn of the millennium.

Tarbat Ness

At the southern entrance to
Dornoch Firth stands one of the
tallest lighthouses in Britain.
Entering the firth by boat can be
a hazard due to the presence of a
shifting sandbank called Gizzen
Briggs. The name is of Norse
origin. In the nearby villages of
Nigg, Shandwick and Hilton of
Cadboll, three ancient carved
stones are said to mark the
graves of three Viking princes
lost in a shipwreck on a local
submerged reef.

Dunrobin Castle

In its magnificent position looking out over the North Sea, there is a touch of the Ruritanian fantasy about Dunrobin Castle, for 700 years the seat of the earls and dukes of Sutherland. Originally a square keep built by Robert, Earl of Sutherland, in 1275, over the centuries it was extended by a tower and hall wing which eventually enclosed a courtyard. Then in the mid-nineteenth century Sir Charles Barry, who built the Houses of Parliament, went to town and gave the castle the Scottish baronial meets Count Dracula look it has today. In 1915, when in use as a naval hospital, much of this latest extension was burnt down, resulting in further reconstruction by Sir Robert Lorimer.

Strath of Kildonan

The River Helmsdale flows
through this far northern valley
of open moor and peat bog,
littered with ancient remains of
brochs, burial places and hut
circles. In the nineteenth
century, Kildonan was the scene
of some of the most notorious
Clearances, initiated by an
Engish liberal 'improver', the
Marquess of Stafford (later
created Duke of Sutherland) and
carried out with brutal efficiency
by his factor, Patrick Sellar. Many
of the 2000 crofters evicted
between 1801 and 1831
emigrated to the Red River
district of Canada, which they
named New Kildonan. In 1868,
gold was discovered in the
Kildonan Burn and a minor gold
rush brought people back to the
strath until the extraction of the
gold proved to be uneconomic.

Berriedale

The village lies at the mouth of
Berriedale Water. The post office,
old smithy and this small lodge
are all decorated with the antlers
of local red deer.

Orkney

The great Scottish writer Edwin Muir spent the first fourteen years of his life on farms in Orkney. Few have described the islands better.

'The Orkney I was born into was a place where there was no great distinction between the ordinary and the fabulous; the lives of living men turned into legend. A man I knew once sailed out in a boat to look for a mermaid, and claimed afterwards that he had talked with her. Fantastic feats of strength were commonly reported. Fairies, or 'fairicks', as they were called, were encountered dancing on the sands on moonlight nights. From people's talk they were small graceful creatures about the size of leprechauns, but pretty, not grotesque. There was no harm in them. All these things have vanished from Orkney in the last fifty years under the pressure of compulsory education.'

EDWIN MUIR, *An Autobiography*

Stenness, Orkney

On a narrow neck of land overlooking the Loch of Harray, the standing stones at Stenness date from around 1800 BC and are almost certainly the remains of a large circle like the nearby Ring of Brodgar. Interpretations of the significance of these monuments (from the religious to the astronomical) vary widely, but while allowing admiration for the skill and dedication of early man in setting them up, standing stones for all their fascination remain little understood. The richest archaeological area in Britain, Orkney can claim three sites of antiquarian interest to every square mile.

Earl's Palace, Orkney

At the far north-western tip of Mainland stand the ruins of the Palace of Birsay, a residence of the early Norse bishops and later Scottish earls of Orkney. It was rebuilt in the late sixteenth century by Earl Robert Stewart as a holiday residence in the manner of Falkland palace.

Orkney

In 1850 a violent storm revealed the remains of a remarkable neolithic village at Skara Brae on the sandy Bay of Skaill. It is thought that the village may have been overwhelmed Pompeii-style by another storm some 4000 years earlier and buried under sand. The result is one of the most extraordinarily well-preserved prehistoric sites in Britain. The wall or dry-stone dyke shown here and the stone slabs that roofed the ruined cottage are examples of the Orcadian tradition of building with stone using techniques similar to those displayed by the inhabitants of Skara Brae.

The Churchill Barrier

During the Second World War, after the sinking of HMS *Royal Oak,* Winston Churchill ordered a series of causeways to be built linking the Orkney mainland with the islands of South Ronaldsay, Lamb Holm, Glimps and Burray and blocking the eastern approaches to the important naval base at Scapa Flow. It was in this same natural harbour that the defeated German fleet had scuttled its ships in 1919. The wrecks seen here and on either side of the causeway belong to the old boom-ships that formed a temporary barrier before the permanent one could be built. On Lamb Holm there is an unusual chapel cleverly constructed out of Nissen huts and scrap metal by Italian prisoners of war who were working on the causeway that once secured Scapa Flow and now offers rapid transport between the oil-rich islands.

The Old Man of Hoy

The second largest island in the Orkney archipelago, Hoy is also the most spectacular. Its impressive sea cliffs on the north-west coast stretch from St John's Head, where they soar over 1000 feet, to the famous Old Man of Hoy. A detached pillar of rock rising sheer from the Pentland Firth, the 450 foot red sandstone stack was first climbed in 1966 and on a clear day can be seen from the mainland of Scotland.

Shetland ponies

When fully grown the Shetland pony stands 3'6" at the shoulder. Their diminutive size and sturdiness formerly made them popular as working ponies in mines and on farms. Bred for generations on the Shetland island of Fetlar off the east coast of Yell, they are now greatly in demand around the world as pets, though as many a child has discovered to its cost their appealing looks often hide less than biddable tempers.

Tongue

In the district of Strathnaver, which once encompassed the whole north-western tip of Scotland, the House of Tongue was formerly the seat of the Reay family, chiefs of Clan Mackay, until the estates were sold in 1829 to the Duke of Sutherland to pay off gambling debts. St Andrew's Church at Tongue was built in 1724 and is the burial place of the Mackay chiefs. The laird's loft is covered in the Mackay tartan.

Loch Eriboll

At the very top of Scotland, this long, fjord-like sea loch runs south into steep mountainous country. Because of its deep water and excellent shelter, it was used as a naval anchorage during the Second World War. It was here in 1945 that German submarines came to surrender to the Allies, which has been taken as confirmation of a seventeenth-century prophecy made by the Brahan Seer that one day a war would come to an end in Loch Eriboll.

Cranstackie

A wild and forbidding mountain wilderness with sombre rock-strewn glens, threateningly perched glacial boulders and dark lochans that provide rewarding sport among brown trout for those who are willing to walk a distance to take their pleasures – there is probably no better place in Scotland for the visitor in search of solitude.

Balnakeil House

This early eighteenth-century farmhouse lies close to the white curving beach of Balnakeil Bay in the far north-west of Scotland. Built on the site of the summer residence of the bishops of Caithness, it stands near to the ruin of Durness Old Church. A seventeenth-century gravestone marked by a skull and crossbones is thought to be that of Donald MacMurchov, a successful local brigand who was buried here in return for the financial assistance he gave to the then Lord Reay, Chief of Mackay, who wanted to rebuild the church, but couldn't afford the expense.

Loch Glencoul

In one of the remotest regions of the north-west Highlands, Loch Glencoul lies to the east of Kylescue and like a Norwegian fjord penetrates deep into the wild and trackless hills. Beyond the head of the loch, Eas-coul-Aulin, the highest waterfall in Britain, drops 658 feet into a lonely glen that can only be reached by boat and on foot, but when the falls are in full spate the magnificent sight is well worth the voyage.

The Callop River

An island of Scots firs marooned in the Callop river, Wester Ross. On its far bank, stark against the sheltering green of the hill, safe in its remoteness, a traditional highland cottage looks towards Beinn Odhar Mhor and Beinn Odhar Bheagg.

Dundonnell House

A pleasing example of eighteenth-century Scottish domestic architecture – plain, modest, symmetrical without being austere – Dundonnell was built in 1769, long after the estate had passed from the MacDonnells of Glengarry to the Mackenzies in the seventeenth century. The house and its remarkable garden stand in a fertile strath below the mighty An Teallach (3500 feet) within earshot of a spate river that rushes through the grounds on its way to join the sea at Little Loch Broom. Developed from an existing walled kitchen garden (with a 1200-year-old yew at its centre) by the Roger brothers, who acquired the estate in 1956, the garden has a strong oriental flavour that is all the more interesting for its Highland setting.

Ullapool

The township of Ullapool on the shores of Loch Broom was founded in 1788 by the British Fisheries Society as a fishing station. The fishing, mainly for herring and white fish, declined in the nineteenth century, but revived during the Second World War. Ullapool, with its fine whitewashed buildings, remains an important centre for the fishing fleet as well as a lively tourist resort.

Lael Forest

Not far from Corrieshalloch Gorge, a spectacular mile-long cleft into which the Measach Falls plunge 200 feet, this attractive cottage on the road to Loch Broom offers bed-and-breakfast accommodation. Clean, comfortable and good value, bed-and-breakfast establishments in Scotland have a deserved reputation for friendliness and offer an opportunity to get to know the local people.

Cuillin Hills, Isle of Skye

The jagged ramparts of the 'Black Cuillins' at the south end of Skye form a six-mile semicircle of black gabbro mountains that offer some of the most exciting rock climbing in Britain. There are at least fifteen peaks that qualify as 'Munros' – that is, over 3000 feet, of which Sgurr Gillean with its pinnacled summit is perhaps the most impressive. From below, the Black Cuillins present a daunting sight. After a visit in 1765, Thomas Gray wrote: 'There are certain scenes that would awe an atheist into belief.' Overlooking the wild and romantic Loch Coruisk, which Sir Walter Scott described in *The Lord of the Isles*, the Cuillins attracted many artists (including J.M.W. Turner) as well as climbers and tourists in the nineteenth century.

Plockton

Just off the main road leading to Kyle of Lochalsh lies the idyllic village of Plockton on the shores of Loch Carron. Established in the eighteenth century as a fishing place, it now supports a crofting community. Warmed by the Gulf Stream – note the palm trees growing on the village street – Plockton is a popular haven with west coast yachtsmen.

Isle of Eigg

A croft on the Inner Hebridean island of Eigg nestles under An Sgurr, a residual block of pitchstone lava, whose oddly shaped peak rises a sheer 300 feet above the high cliff-like contour. A cave at the southern tip of Eigg was the scene of a clan massacre in 1577, when the Macleods of Skye lit a fire at the cave's entrance and suffocated 200 MacDonalds hiding inside. Sir Walter Scott, on a visit to Eigg in 1814, claimed to have 'brought off a skull from among the numerous specimens of mortality which the cavern afforded.' In the bay of Laig, on the island's west coast, the Singing Sands emit a strange keening sound when trodden underfoot, performing best around sunset, but only if the fine quartz sand is dry.

Camusdarroch

The silver sands of Morar are famed in poetry and song, but I would find it difficult to write even a caption about the beach at Camusdarroch on any other than a personal note. For it was here that I spent many idyllic summers as a child, usually in the company of a large happy band of cousins. We would stay out all day on the beach, whatever the weather, swimming in the cold green Minch, poring over rock pools, hunting for cowrie shells along the tide marks and tobogganing down the steep gleaming white dunes. There were games and fights and picnics, which I remember for the taste of floury white baps filled with strawberry jam that somehow always ended up gritty with sand. The beach was used as a location for the film *Local Hero*, which managed to capture some of Camusdarroch's magic without stealing it.

Arisaig

There is no more determined colonist in Scotland than the *Rhododendron ponticum,* once admired as an exotic import and now commonly regarded as a destructive and remorselessly advancing weed. Though never described as bonny, its distinctive mauve trusses have become as familiar and accepted a part of the colour scheme of the Highland landscape as the yellow broom or purple heather.

Glenfinnan

At the head of Loch Shiel, on the west coast's 'Road to the Isles', stands the Glenfinnan Monument commemorating the '45 Jacobite Rising. It was here on 19 August 1745 that Prince Charles Edward's standard was raised as a rallying call to the Highland clans. The arrival at Glenfinnan of Lochiel and his clansmen convinced others that the attempt to win back the British Crown for the Stuarts was a feasible proposition. The figure on top of the column represents a Highlander (by Greenshields) and was erected in 1815 by Macdonald of Glenaladale, a descendant of one of the prince's most loyal followers. The Glenfinnan Gathering and Highland Games are held in this romantic spot every year on the Saturday in August that falls nearest to the anniversary of the Rising.

Achnacarry House

The seat of the Camerons of Lochiel, chiefs of Clan Cameron, since the seventeenth century, Achnacarry House, which lies among the wooded hills of Lochaber, was built in 1802 to replace the former castle destroyed by the Duke of Cumberland in 1746. A long line of remarkable chiefs has made 'Lochiel' one of the most famous of chiefly titles. It was Donald Cameron, known as the 'Gentle Lochiel', who despite deep misgivings about their chances of success told Prince Charles Edward, soon after he landed from France in the spring of 1745, 'I'll share the fate of my Prince, and so shall every man over whom nature or fortune has given me power.' On this momentous decision depended the fate of the Highlands, for without Lochiel's support the other chiefs would not have taken up arms. Lochiel was badly wounded at Culloden but escaped to France where he died in exile two years later. His family returned after being amnestied in 1784.

The Garden House, Achnacarry

'A beautiful summerhouse that stood in the pleasure garden was also set on fire and everything valuable was burnt or destroyed', runs a contemporary account of the wasting of Achnacarry. The English troops, 320 men of Bligh's Regiment, dragged Lochiel's old gardener and cook from their hiding place and flogged them until their backs were raw to make them reveal where their chief's silver and jewellery were buried in the grounds. Which they would not do. Supposedly Lochiel and some of his men watched Achnacarry burn from the hills and saw the soldiers trample the avenue of beach saplings he had himself planted the year before. The surviving trees grown to maturity still line the drive up to the house.

Stag in velvet

The legendary Damh Mor, the great stag who lived for 200 years in Badenoch, was a mythical beast. Most stags reach maturity at twelve; their life histories (the stag pictured here in velvet is five years old) can be read in the growth and decline of their antlers. Although the open season runs from 1 July to 20 October, stags are not usually stalked until late August or early September when newly formed antlers are clear of their furry covering and the beasts are in prime condition. Cast antlers are eaten by both hinds and stags, probably for their calcium content. In autumn, during the rut or mating season, stags become fiercely territorial and the Highland glens echo to their roaring and the clash of duelling antlers.

Creag Meagaidh

At the western end of the Monadhliath Mountains above Loch Laggan, Creag Meagaidh (3700 feet) and the stern wild beauty of the surrounding countryside are of great interest to geologists, as an example of the peaks and plateaus left by the scouring action of glaciers during the last Ice Age.

Macpherson of Glentruim

Restored from a ruin by Ewan Macpherson's great-grandfather, Glentruim House in Badenoch looks out over Invernahavon, where in 1370 the Camerons and the Macphersons (who belonged to the powerful federation of northern clans known as Clan Chattan) fought a bloody but indecisive battle. The feud between Clan Chattan and the Camerons continued, reaching its climax at the Battle of North Inch in Perth in 1396, which was immortalized by Sir Walter Scott in *The Fair Maid of Perth*. Chieftain of a cadet branch of the Macphersons, Ewan, the present laird of Glentruim, broke with tradition when he came to live in the house by giving his wife the freedom of the smoking room (*left*), where no woman it seems had ever set foot. As can be seen, the feminine influence has not had too noticeable an effect on this comfortably male preserve.

Loch Laggan

Were it not for the rain, we might well be referring to this part of the central Highlands as 'Royal Lagganside'. Built in 1840 by the Duke of Abercorn, Ardverikie House stands on the southern shore of Loch Laggan. It was visited by Queen Victoria on one of her first trips to the Highlands. She gave serious consideration to buying the house as a 'Highland home', but was put off by the 'persistent rain' which she noted tended to 'come down in sheets'. It rained all the days of her stay. She looked further east and plumped for Balmoral.

Dalwhinnie

In desolate country near the
north end of Loch Ericht, the
somewhat bleak village of
Dalwhinnie can at least boast
the highest distillery in Scotland
(1180 feet). A favourite rallying
place of the clans – Dalwhinnie
in Gaelic means 'dell of the
meeting' – it was here in 1745
that General Cope declined to
intercept Prince Charlie and his
Highland army, judging that
he could not win against a
guerrilla force on its native
territory. His failure to engage
the clans left open to them the
road to Edinburgh and the
Lowlands and did not prevent
his own defeat at Prestonpans.
Ironically, a year later, the Prince
came back through the area as a
fugitive and hid for a time with
Cluny Macpherson in Cluny's
Cage on the west shore of Loch
Ericht.

Ben Nevis

Best known for being Britain's highest mountain, Ben Nevis (4406 feet) rarely looks as impressive as it should, having neither peak nor clearly defined summit. It rears above Fort William rather like an elephant's head; you can in fact drive a car to the top. A hill walker's and climber's mountain, Ben Nevis has a precipitous north face, best seen from Corpach or Spean Bridge, which presents a challenge even to experienced climbers. Because it stands close to the sea, climatic conditions on Nevis are changeable, often producing a thick cloud cover which can be hazardous but from the ground helps preserve the mountain's limited mystique.

Falls of Dochart

The highland village of Killin lies at the western end of Loch Tay, into which the River Dochart tumbles in a series of falls and rapids that can look quite impressive during a spate. The Dochart is spanned by a bridge dating from around 1730 and on a small island just below the falls lies the burial place of the Clan Macnab. The Macnabs were closely associated with the Killin district until an old prophecy that 'when a great storm blew the branch of a pine tree against the trunk of another, and grafted itself onto the trunk, the Macnabs would lose their lands' was fulfilled; in 1828 the old clan lands were sold off for debt and the family emigrated to Canada.

Kilchurn Castle

On a former island at the north-eastern end of Loch Awe in Argyll, the original keep of Kilchurn was built by Sir Colin Campbell of Glenorchy, the founder of the powerful Breadalbane family, in 1440. As late as 1900, the Marquess of Breadalbane could ride a hundred miles in a straight line from east to west without leaving his land. The castle was added to in the sixteenth and seventeenth centuries and offered by the anti-Jacobite Breadalbanes as a garrison for Hanoverian troops in 1746. The top of one of the towers was blown down in the same gale of 1879 that destroyed the Tay Bridge. The now ruinous castle enjoys a wonderful setting at the head of Glenorchy under the shadow of Ben Cruachan.

Castle Stalker

The ancient home of the Stewarts of Appin, Castle Stalker (a corruption of 'Stalcair' from the Gaelic for 'hunter') rises impressively from its rocky islet in Loch Linnhe. Built in the thirteenth century as one of a series of fortresses on the west coast of Argyll, it has been well restored and is still lived in during the summer months by its owners. Appin is perhaps best known for the unsolved murder of the Red Fox, Colin Campbell of Glenure, in 1752; the story plays a dramatic part in Robert Louis Stevenson's novel *Kidnapped*. One of the Stewarts of Appin, James of the Glens, was accused of the deed, tried at Inveraray by a Campbell judge and jury and hanged near Ballchulish, where there is a tablet erected to his memory.

Loch Fyne

On the main road into Inveraray, by Loch Fyne, several elegant eighteenth-century bridges such as this hint at the combination of extraordinary wealth and single-minded planning that created this town. Inveraray is at the heart of 'Campbell country', the domain of the dukes of Argyll; the 6th Duke, who died in 1839 without issue, is reputed to have gambled away £4 million, as well as sired 398 illegitimate children, which may go some way towards explaining why Campbells can be found on every corner of the globe.

Loch Fyne

In the late 1970s John Noble, owner of Ardkinglas Estate, and Andrew Lane, marine fish farmer, started raising oysters in upper Loch Fyne. Local conditions appeared ideal: the water was pure and unpolluted, the estuarine head of the loch fertile; and the perfect balance of fresh and salt water ensured good growth and fine flavour. Large quantities of old oyster shells found on the foreshore indicated the existence of much earlier oyster beds. In the eighteenth and nineteenth centuries, oysters were highly popular in Scotland. They were sold in Glasgow and Edinburgh both in special cellars or 'howfs' and by oyster lassies, whose street cry 'wha'll o caller oysters' vended 100,000 oysters daily in Edinburgh alone. The bold but simple aim of Loch Fyne Oysters Ltd, to reverse the dwindling market for oysters in Britain and turn what had become an exclusive luxury into an everyday delicacy for all, has met with a deserved and worldwide success.

Inveraray

Inveraray was created a royal burgh in 1648, four years after a significant part of the village was destroyed by the Marquess of Montrose during his remarkable foray into Campbell country. The present small town, the most architecturally distinguished in the Highlands, was designed in the mid-eighteenth century by Roger Morris and William Adam, both of whom died before realizing their plans, which were then carried out by Robert Mylne, with John Adam (William's elder son) supervising the works. Many of the buildings, including the fine town house pictured here, were completed by 1751. The courthouse overlooking Loch Fyne was not built until 1820; together with the town jail, it has recently been turned into a museum. It was at the inn in Inveraray that Dr Johnson, ordering his first glass of whisky, cried: 'Come, let me know what it is that makes a Scotchman happy!'

Inveraray Castle

A resplendent view of the home
of the dukes of Argyll from across
Loch Fyne. The present castle at
Inveraray was started by Roger
Morris and William Adam in
1743 on the instructions of the
3rd Duke, whose bold vision
of a new residence included
sweeping away the existing castle
and town of Inveraray clustered
about its walls. Robert Mylne
completed the castle in the
1770s, close to the date of the
visit by Boswell and Johnson,
who were 'much struck by the
grandeur and elegance of this
princely seat'. Among the earliest
examples of neo-gothic architecture in Britain, Inveraray's
towers and upper storey were
heavily Victorianized, but behind
the facade of this extraordinary
mock-castle lies one of the finest
classical eighteenth-century
interiors in Scotland, if not
Europe.

Auchindrain

The interior of Bell Pol's house at Auchindrain gives the visitor to this open-air folk museum an idea of life on a farming township in the eighteenth and early nineteenth centuries. The restored village consists of stone-built houses and farm buildings – byres, barns, stable, smithy and corn kilns – grouped in the traditional way, each dwelling surrounded by its own plot of land. Auchindrain and its strip system farm were held on a joint tenure basis and its inhabitants paid a communal rent to the Duke of Argyll at nearby Inveraray.

Loch Sween

'The poorer tenants, who have no winter parks, are under the necessity of keeping the cattle under the same roof with themselves during night; and often are obliged to keep them alive with the meal designed for their families. The cows are often forced, through want of other food, to have recourse to the shores, and feed on the sea-plants at low water: by instinct they will, at ebb of tide, hasten from the moors, notwithstanding they are not within sight of the sea.'

THOMAS PENNANT,
17 July 1772

Isle of Gigha

A small Atlantic island lying between Islay and the Kintyre peninsula, Gigha (from the Norse, 'Isle of God') is one of the most fertile of the Inner Hebrides. The island was bought in 1944 by Sir James Horlick, who created around Achamore House a woodland garden that has few equals on the west coast for sheer enchantment. Protected from the Atlantic gales by shelter belts of sycamores, the garden's collection of rare, tender and sub-tropical plants was donated by Sir James in 1962 to the National Trust for Scotland.

Castle Lachlan

The ruins of old Castle Lachlan, overlooking Lachlan Bay on the shores of Loch Fyne, date from the early Middle Ages, though most of the structure is sixteenth-century. The castle was formerly the stronghold of the Maclachlans of that Ilk, but was abandoned after being bombarded from the sea by a Government ship in 1746. The Maclachlans were loyal Jacobites and suffered heavy losses at Culloden, including the death of their chief, Lachlan Maclachlan. The story goes that as the surviving clansmen straggled back from Culloden, the dead chief's riderless horse ran from the battlefield and swam home across Loch Fyne bringing first news of the disaster. According to the present chief of Clan Lachlan, who lives in the new and nearby Castle Lachlan, built in the early part of the last century, there have been numerous sightings of the riderless horse swimming the loch of a cold and moonlit night.

Benmore

At the head of Loch Eck, the slender Victorian towers of Benmore House rise among the stately conifers of Younger Botanic Garden, an important annexe of the Royal Botanic Garden in Edinburgh. The house and its remarkable collection of rare trees and flowering shrubs (there are over 250 species of rhododendron) was presented to the Forestry Commission in 1928 by the owner, G.H. Younger, and lies within the Argyll National Forest Park. An avenue of spectacular California redwoods planted in 1865 leads the unsuspecting visitor to Benmore into an extraordinarily fertile and exotic world that can be experienced in many of the great west coast gardens, warmed by the Gulf Stream and a mild climate.

The Creggans

When Mary Queen of Scots landed at Creggans some 400 years ago, the bar at the Creggans Inn (*left*) wasn't as well stocked as it is today and she spent an uncomfortable night as the guest of the local laird, MacPhunn of Dripp. A later MacPhunn, fallen on hard times, was hanged for murder at Inveraray, but tradition has it that his wife, while bringing his body home to Strachur, managed to revive him with a mixture of whisky and mother's milk as they were being rowed back across Loch Fyne through the dawn mists (*right*). In those days you couldn't be hanged twice for the same crime and the ne'er-do-well MacPhunn, known as 'Half-hung Archie', lived to a ripe old age. The Creggans Inn's own malt, 'Old MacPhunn', is named after him and is the chief ingredient of a lethal cocktail – three parts whisky, one part cream – called a 'Noose-loosener'.

Pipe-Major Niall Campbell

Niall Campbell was born in the village of Strachur on Loch Fyne in 1918 and by the age of twelve was playing the bagpipes. During the Second World War he served as a piper under Pipe-Major Ronnie MacCallum in the 11th Battalion of the Argyll and Sutherland Highlanders. In 1967, with the aim of keeping alive the tradition of piping locally, he started tutoring children in the pipes in the parish of Strachur and Strathlachlan. Twelve years later he was appointed full-time instructor for all schools in the Cowal district and in 1988 was awarded the British Empire Medal for 'Service to Piping'.

The River Kinglas, Loch Fyne

Another Loch Fynesider, Neil Munro (1864–1930), author of the 'Para Handy' tales, wrote this of the pipes in *John Splendid*:

'On a sudden there rose away before us towards the mouth of the glen the sound of a bagpipe. It came on the tranquil air with no break in its uproar, and after a preparatory tuning it broke into an air called "Cogadh no Sith" – an ancient braggart pibroch made by one Macruimen of the Isle of Skye – a tune that was commonly used by the Campbells as a night retreat or tattoo.

'My heart filled with the strain. It gave me not only the simple illusion that I saw again the regimentals of my native country – many a friend and comrade among them in the shelter of the Castle of Inverlochy – but it roused in me a spirit, very antique, very religious and moving too, as the music of his own land must in every honest Gael.

'"Cruachan for ever!" I said lightly to McIver, though my heart was full.'

Strachur Park

This handsome eighteenth-century bridge leads from a square of farm buildings to Strachur House. An attractive Georgian mansion, Strachur was built in 1783 by General John Campbell, who on his return from fighting on the British side in the American War of Independence decided to replace his old family home at Succoth, the ancient seat of the MacArthur Campbells, with a more modern structure. The general, a kinsman of the Duke of Argyll, may have sought the advice of some of the renowned architects working at the time at Inveraray, but there is no documentary evidence to support this. He also laid out a park at Strachur, deploying trees, mostly beeches and Scots firs, according to the battle plans of his favourite campaigns.

'Rest and be thankful'

The road seen here meandering along Glen Croe climbs from Arrochar, zigzagging through grand Highland scenery, to a watershed of 860 feet, where a rough stone seat inscribed with the words 'Rest and be thankful' has given its name to the pass. The construction of the road was ordered by General Cope in 1744 and built by Caulfield between 1746 and 1748, whose workmen may have left the inscription.

Loch Lomond

Pleasure boats have been cruising Loch Lomond, the largest inland water in Great Britain, since Sir Walter Scott awakened an interest in the Trossachs and the Western Highlands. The last paddle steamer to be built in Europe, the 'Lady of the Loch' is being refitted at Balloch before resuming summer sailings that traditionally include stops at some of the loch's thirty wooded islands. The largest of these is Inchmurrin (Isle of Spears), where visitors can spend time brooding over the ruins of Lennox Castle. Despite the proximity of Glasgow and relentless commercialization, the banks and braes of Loch Lomond remain as bonny as the famous song, written by a Jacobite imprisoned in Carlisle, would have us believe.

Central Station, Glasgow

'There is a Transatlantic alertness
about Glasgow which no city in
England possesses . . . She is
Scotland's anchor to reality.
Lacking her, Scotland would be a
backward country lost in poetic
memories and at an enmity with
an age in which she was playing
no part. Glasgow, facing west to
the new trade-ways of the world,
rose after the Union, calling to
Highlands and Lowlands to forget
old scores and to take a hand in
the building of that new world
which was to begin on a Sabbath
afternoon in the spring of 1765
when James Watt walked over
Glasgow Green occupied with
sinful weekday thoughts. The
new age began sinfully on that
Sabbath, for James Watt had
solved the problem of the
separate condenser; and as he
walked over Glasgow Green a
changed world lay pregnant in
his brain: a world of steel and
iron, tall chimneys and speed.'

H.V. MORTON,
In Search of Scotland

The Necropolis, Glasgow

On a wooded hill above the cathedral, across the Bridge of Sighs, lies the Necropolis, the graveyard of the Merchant's House of Glasgow. Reminiscent of the Père-la-Chaise cemetery in Paris, it was opened in 1832 by Provost James Ewing and contains gloriously sombre imitations of architectural styles from all over the world as each Glasgow merchant buried there had his tomb built in the manner of the place where he had made his money.

City Centre, Glasgow

Few would say that Glasgow is a romantic city, and yet . . . here is how Compton Mackenzie saw it and I can't help thinking that most Glaswegians have at some time shared his beatific vision, not necessarily on a Saturday night.

'A few weeks ago upon the Campsie Fells I gazed down at Glasgow. From a mass of dark cloud the sun, himself obscured from where I stood, sloped his golden ladders into that rain-washed city, which lay with all her towers and tenements and sparkling roofs, like a vision of heavenly habitations. I have looked down over Athens. I have looked down over Rome. With beauty unparagoned the glory and the grandeur of the past have been spread before my eyes; but in that sight of Glasgow something was added which neither Rome nor Athens could give – the glory and the grandeur of the future, and the beating heart of a nation.'

SIR COMPTON MACKENZIE, 1932

The River Doon

Ye flowery banks o' bonnie Doon,
How can ye bloom sae fair;
How can ye chant, ye little birds,
And I sae fu' o' care?

The steep and wooded banks of the River Doon that Robert Burns celebrated in the above well-known song can be found some way downstream from the view here, which shows the more rugged side of Burns Country. The river comes at last to the sea, after passing under the Auld Brig o' Doon, a few miles west of Alloway, where Scotland's greatest poet was born on 25 January 1759.

Drumlanrig Castle

Among the hills of Dumfries-shire, the rose-red castle of Drumlanrig, undoubtedly one of the loveliest houses in Scotland, was built of local sandstone on the site of an ancient Douglas fort between 1679 and 1690 for the 1st Duke of Queensberry. Executed by James Smith, working with plans drawn up by the great Sir William Bruce, Drumlanrig represents a departure from the mediaeval style towards a Renaissance concept that nonetheless remains peculiarly Scottish in feeling. The Queensberry titles later merged with those of the Buccleuchs, a family that over the centuries has managed its vast estates with enlightened responsibility, often pioneering new trends in forestry, farming and conservation. The fact that Drumlanrig houses the greatest private collection of paintings, furniture, china and silver in Scotland owes not a little to this skill.

Sweetheart Abbey

One of the most impressive monastic ruins in Scotland, this Cistercian abbey of red sandstone was built in 1273 by Devorguilla, mother of King John Balliol. When her husband John Balliol the elder died, Devorguilla became a rich and powerful woman with castles and estates in England and Normandy, but was left broken-hearted. She founded Balliol College, Oxford in her husband's memory and kept his embalmed heart in an ivory and silver casket which was buried with her in front of the abbey's high altar when she died aged eighty. From their tomb known as 'Dulce Cor' the abbey took its name, and the English language supposedly gained the endearment 'sweetheart'.

Caerlaverock Castle

Remarkable for its triangular shape and moat that is still water-filled, Caerlaverock ranks high among Scotland's great castles for beauty and interest. A stronghold of the Maxwells, later earls of Nithsdale, who were wardens of the western march between Scotland and England, the castle dates from around 1290 and has had an eventful history. Captured by Edward I in 1301, eleven years later it was won back by Sir Eustace Maxwell, a supporter of Robert the Bruce, only to fall to the English again; it changed hands a number of times before, in 1640, after a thirteen-week siege, it was laid to ruin by the Covenanters. Behind its massive defensive walls and drum towers (fourteenth- to fifteenth-century) lie the remains of an extra-ordinarily elegant Renaissance interior of 1634, built by the 1st Earl and known as 'Lord Nithsdale's Daintie Fabrick' but doomed to be destroyed within six years of its completion.

SELECTED BIBLIOGRAPHY

Brinsley Burbidge and Fay Young, *The Scottish Garden*, Mowbray House, 1989
David Daiches, *Sir Walter Scott*, Thames and Hudson, 1971
Hubert Fenwick, *Scottish Baronial Houses*, Robert Hale, 1986
John Fleming, *Scottish Country Houses and Gardens*, Country Life, 1954
Sheila Forman, *Scottish Country Houses and Castles*, George Outram, 1967
Lewis Ann Garner, *The Best Fishing in Scotland*, Lochar, 1990
Ian C. Hannah, *The Story of Scotland in Stone*, Oliver and Boyd, 1934
Christian Hesketh, *Tartans*, Octopus, 1972
Fred Holliday, edited, *Wildlife of Scotland*, Macmillan, 1979
Fitzroy Maclean, *A Concise History of Scotland*, Thames and Hudson, 1970
Sir Iain Moncreiffe of that Ilk, *The Highland Clans*, Barrie and Jenkins, 1982
H.V. Morton, *In Search of Scotland*, Methuen, 1929
Edwin Muir, *An Autobiography*, Hogarth Press, 1954
Robert J. Naismith, *Buildings of the Scottish Countryside*, Gollancz, 1989
Harold Orel, edited, *The Scottish World*, Thames and Hudson, 1981
Anna Ritchie, Series Editor, *Exploring Scotland's Heritage*, HMSO, 1985
Otta F. Swire, *The Highlands and their Legends*, Oliver and Boyd, 1963
Christopher Tabraham, *Scottish Castles and Fortifications*, HMSO, 1986
Gerald Warner, *Homelands of the Clans*, Collins, 1980
A.J. Youngson, *Beyond the Highland Line*, Collins, 1974

INDEX